Fantastic
ANIMAL
FEATURES

Written by
Heather Parker

STECK-VAUGHN
ELEMENTARY · SECONDARY · ADULT · LIBRARY
A Harcourt Classroom Education Company

www.steck-vaughn.com

Contents

Chapter 1

Aren't Some Animals Amazing?

If you've ever been to a zoo, visited an aquarium, or looked through a book about animals, you've probably come across some very strange-looking creatures. Maybe you've wondered why an animal had such an odd nose, or weird fingers, or parts you couldn't even name!

The truth is, there are reasons for all of these strange features. In fact, many animal features give clues about how an animal lives, or what its home is like, or maybe even what it eats.

The manatee is a mammal that lives in shallow water.

Chapter 2

Goosefish and Frogfish Go Fishing

The ocean is filled with many kinds of fish. In fact, there are over 20,000 different kinds of fish that we know of, and new fish are found all the time. Some live in warm, shallow waters, while some live in deep, dark, cold waters. Two kinds of fish that live in different parts of the ocean are the goosefish and the frogfish.

The goosefish and the frogfish look very different from each other. One is long and large. The other is short and **spiny**. One looks mean. The other wears a pout. One is dark and drab. The other can be as colorful as any creature in the ocean.

As different as they are, the goosefish and the frogfish share some fantastic features. One of these features sets them apart from other fish. It's what makes these two ocean creatures fish that go fishing.

The goosefish is a large, weird-looking creature. Its head is about as wide as its body, but much bigger. The goosefish is usually about 3 feet (91 centimeters) long and weighs as much as a small three-year-old child.

The goosefish has an odd face with eyes near the top of its head. It has four rows of teeth. It even has teeth on the roof of its mouth. With its huge mouth and large lower jaw, the goosefish looks very mean. This fish may not be mean, but it has a fierce appetite.

A goosefish lives in deep, dark water.

A brightly colored frogfish

The frogfish is odd looking in a different way. Some people think it looks like a frog. It is small enough to hold in your hands. It grows to only about 5 inches (13 centimeters). The **pectoral fins**, which are found on the fish's chest, spread out like many fingers on stubby arms. It uses these strange, finger-like pectoral fins to walk along the shallow bottom of the ocean.

The frogfish is covered with nubs of skin. Its face is hard to see with all these nubs. It has small eyes. Like the goosefish, it has a huge mouth.

The frogfish has an amazing ability. It can change its color to blend in with the colorful **coral**, rock, or seaweed around it. It might become bright orange, purple and yellow, or almost any color of the rainbow, to match its **environment**. Its **camouflage** helps the frogfish hide from its **prey**. Camouflage also keeps it hidden from sea creatures that could attack. The camouflage helps it survive.

The frogfish lives in warm, shallow waters where there are many rocky surfaces and coral. The nubby, uneven skin of the frogfish is part of its camouflage. Next to the rough rocks, the frogfish seems to disappear.

The goosefish does not change its color. It lives in colder parts of the ocean where its environment is darker and not so colorful. There, its dark, drab color blends with its surroundings and keeps many fish from seeing it.

Both the frogfish and the goosefish are **anglers**. Anglers go fishing, just as people do. But they have a special way of catching fish and a fantastic feature to help them.

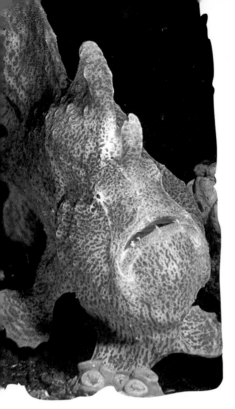
The frogfish waits to catch its dinner.

Animal features often change over hundreds or thousands of years. The changes usually help an animal survive better in its environment.

Over many years, the **dorsal fins** (which are found on the fish's back) of the goosefish and frogfish have changed. The goosefish and the frogfish use what is left of their dorsal fins to trap prey. As they wait, they jiggle this fantastic feature almost like a fishing pole. To other fish, the moving spine looks like something to eat. When the other fish come near, the huge mouth of the angler opens wide to catch them.

The goosefish and the frogfish can gulp down prey as big as themselves. Their teeth help move the extra large meal into their stomachs. Then, their stomachs expand to make room for the feast.

Chapter 3

An Unusual Bird

We usually think of birds as feathered creatures that fly. They are graceful and often beautiful. But not the hoatzin (hoh AT sihn)!

The hoatzin is an awkward looking bird. It wears a crown of rusty-brown feathers. This bird smells so bad that people who live near it call it a stinkbird.

The hoatzin's head is small for its body. Its face is covered not with feathers, but with blue skin. It has long claws on its big feet, and its wings are very short.

The hoatzin doesn't use its short wings much. In fact, it's a poor flyer. It is **arboreal**, so it spends most of its time in trees.

Long claws help the hoatzin live in trees.

The hoatzin spends more time moving around in trees than it spends flying. It has a very strong, curved beak. Its long claws can wrap around branches. It uses its beak and claws to climb.

A baby hoatzin has a special feature to help it climb. When it begins life, its wings are not ready for even the shortest flight. But the baby hoatzin has two claws at the bend of each wing. The young bird uses these front claws to grip branches.

The young hoatzin has another unusual ability. If danger is near, it can dive from the branches, plunge into the water, and swim away to safety.

Hoatzins eat leaves, flowers, and fruits. They nest in groups and care for their young together. They are found in South America.

A hoatzin has blue skin on its head.

Chapter 4

The Tiny Tarsier

After one look you might not guess that the tarsier is related to monkeys and apes. In fact, it is related to over two hundred other kinds of animals called **primates**. Believe it or not, humans are primates! All primates are also part of an even larger group of animals called mammals.

The tarsier is one mammal whose many odd features make it special. Its ears are large, and its eyes are huge. Its body is very small, only 3 to 6 inches (8–15 centimeters) long. It has very long, bony fingers and toes and a very long tail. These strange features are matched to the tarsier's way of life.

The tarsier's huge eyes look shocked and frightened. No other mammal has eyes as big.

Tarsiers have large eyes to see at night.

The tarsier needs large eyes for a reason. It is **nocturnal**. The tarsier comes out after dark. Its extra-large eyes help it see when there is almost no light. The tarsier also has good hearing. Good night vision and good hearing are important to the tarsier as it hunts.

The tarsier's odd-looking fingers and toes are also very important to its way of life. Tarsiers are arboreal. When they are not hunting, they stay up in trees. Their toes are very long and jointed like their fingers. Their fingers are thin and knobby, but the tips have flat, wide cushions. These fingers and toes help the tarsier grab branches and tree trunks as it climbs. The tarsier also has strong hind legs. It is an excellent jumper. It uses its strong legs to jump between branches and trees easily.

The tarsier has an unusual way of jumping. It actually pushes off from a tree backwards. It pulls its arms and legs in close to its body. Then it quickly turns around in the air before landing. Before it jumps, it can turn its head so far around that it can look almost directly behind itself.

The tarsier makes good use of its long tail, too. The tail helps it keep its balance and direction when jumping. The tail also helps it stay safely in place in the trees when resting.

Like most mammals, the baby tarsier is born covered with hair. It has a strong grip from the very beginning. It uses its strong fingers and toes to hold fast to its mother's stomach after birth.

Tarsiers live in the rain forests of the Philippines and Indonesia. They eat only meat (mostly insects and lizards) and live alone or with their young. They can live eight or more years.

Tarsiers move by jumping from tree to tree.

Chapter 5

A Leggy Lizard

There are many kinds of lizards around the world. They often live in the trees or on the ground. Some live in the water. The basilisk lizard is often in the water, and it may seem like any other lizard at first glance. But if you look again, you'll see that it is built to perform some amazing feats. A close look at the basilisk's features shows where it gets its special talents.

The basilisk grows to about 28 inches (71 centimeters) in

length. That's about as long as a small wagon. Its long tail makes up most of its length. Its front legs are small. Its back legs are long and strong, and its back feet are webbed.

In the basilisk's hind legs and feet, we find the keys to its unusual abilities. Like other animals with webbed feet, the basilisk is a swimmer. With its strong back legs, it can swim fast enough to come right up out of the water. It then seems to race across the water on its two webbed feet.

When the basilisk moves across the water this way, it is not actually on top of the water. In fact, one foot at a time is under the water. As it quickly pushes its webbed feet down against the water, little puffs of air are caught underneath them. This air acts like life jackets under its feet. It keeps the basilisk from sinking.

Basilisk lizards live in trees.

Basilisks run on land or water to escape danger.

Basilisks also use their hind legs for running on the ground. They run very fast. The basilisk lives in the trees, usually close to water. When danger is near, this fantastic lizard uses its running and swimming talents to escape.

Basilisks look scary. Male basilisks have a jagged spiny bone that runs from their heads to their tails, just like a dragon. Basilisks may look deadly, but they are not.

Like many other lizards, basilisks like hot, humid weather. They live in tropical areas from Mexico to Central America.

Chapter 6

Hidden Insects

There are more kinds of insects than any other kind of animal. The walking stick and walking leaf insects will amaze anyone lucky enough to see them. These insects are some of nature's

This insect looks like a brown leaf.

most perfectly camouflaged creatures.

Camouflage is present in many kinds of animals. Some animals can change their colors. Others are shaped or colored to look like plants, rocks, or other places where they live.

Walking sticks and walking leaf insects have a special shape and color that helps camouflage them. They are shaped and colored to blend in with their environment. They look just like stems, leaves, or twigs. Most are shades of green or brown.

Walking sticks look like plant stems because they have long, thin, straight bodies. Their legs are sometimes as thin as hair.

This camouflage is very important to walking sticks. Most of them have no wings. Unlike insects that fly, a walking stick cannot quickly escape danger. Its best defense is not to be seen by a **predator** that might eat it. Its camouflage keeps it hidden and helps it survive.

Some walking sticks have another form of defense. If frightened, they can give off a terrible odor. This can help keep a hungry predator away.

Most walking sticks are active at night.

Walking leaves look like leaves that have been eaten or torn. Their legs and even their wings look like parts of leaves. They can be bright green, like a spring leaf, or orange, or brown, like changing or drying leaves. Only a close look, or the insect's sudden movement, will tell that they are not part of a plant. They can easily stay hidden from predators.

This amazing insect even begins life in a protective camouflage. The mother leaf insect lays eggs that look just like seeds. Afterwards, she leaves the eggs to hatch. The seed camouflage helps protect the eggs from predators, such as other insects and animals.

Walking leaves have mouth parts that chew leaves.

This walking leaf looks like an old leaf.

There are many kinds of stick and leaf insects, and they stand out in the huge world of insects. Some are very large. Walking sticks can grow to be about 14 inches (36 centimeters) in length, longer than a ruler. This is the longest known insect in the world. Leaf insects grow to about 3 inches (8 centimeters). Unlike many insects that eat other insects or insect eggs to survive, walking sticks and walking leaves eat only plants. They live mostly in humid and warm areas.

Chapter 7

The Platypus Puzzle

Most mammals live on land. A few, like whales and dolphins, live in water. But **semiaquatic** mammals spend time in both environments. The platypus is a semiaquatic mammal. The odd features of the platypus allow it to live both on land and in water.

The platypus is a puzzle of amazing animal features that don't seem to fit together. It has fur and a tail like a beaver. The platypus has claws, but it also has webbed feet and a bill like a duck. Some of these features tell us that the platypus lives on land. Others tell us that it is a creature of the water.

The platypus has short, thick fur to protect it from cold water.

The front feet pull the platypus through the water as it swims.

Like many mammals, the platypus spends most of its time on land. Since it finds its food underwater, it always lives right next to water. It makes its home in a tunnel alongside a river, stream, or lake.

The platypus has claws on all four feet, but its feet are also webbed, like a duck's feet. Webs stretch between the claws of its back feet. The amazing front feet of the platypus change to fit its needs. On land, only claws can be seen. But underwater, wide webs fold out from under these claws. The front feet of the platypus do most of the swimming work. Its back legs and wide tail are used for steering.

Other features of the platypus change, too. On land, the platypus has small eyes and hidden ears. Underwater, skin covers up its eyes and ears. It cannot see or hear while it swims.

Instead, a special feature helps it find its way around. In place of a nose, the platypus has a special, soft snout shaped like a duck's bill. This is what it uses to find its way around underwater. It also searches for food with its snout. It pushes into the mud for small water creatures. On land, the platypus uses its claws to help with digging its tunnel and with the building of a nest for its young.

A bill helps the platypus find and scoop up food.

The female platypus uses wet plants to build a nest in the tunnel far from its opening. There she lays her eggs and waits for up to ten days for them to hatch. She holds the eggs close to her body with her tail so that they stay warm. She holds her babies this way after they are born, too.

A newborn platypus is tiny, no bigger than a person's thumb. It has no hair and cannot swim. Like other mammals, the young platypus lives on its mother's milk. Unlike other mammals, the platypus is hatched from an egg. This is very unusual. Most mammals do not come into the world as eggs, but as live babies.

The platypus is an unusual mammal in another way. The male is **venomous**. Behind his back feet are pockets of poison. The male platypus can strike and even kill enemies with his poison.

The platypus grows to about 20 inches (51 centimeters) long. That's about as big as a small cat. It lives only in Australia.

Chapter 8

A Flat Frog

Do you know the difference between a frog and a toad? Most frogs have smooth skin and long, strong back legs for leaping. Toads have bumpy, dry skin and shorter legs. Many frogs have webbed feet for swimming. But toads usually live on land. The surinam toad is really a special kind of frog. It is **aquatic**, so it lives completely in water.

This special frog has many weird features that help it survive in the water. Like other frogs, it has strong back legs. These feet are webbed. Both features help make the surinam toad a strong swimmer.

The surinam toad's head is shaped like a triangle.

The surinam toad looks like a brown, flat rock.

The front legs of this frog look very small and feeble. These legs are like hands with fingertips. The surinam toad stretches its fingertips to feel for food at the bottom of the river.

The surinam toad catches its food and eats in a very special way. The surinam toad has no tongue, so it uses its fingertips instead. Most frogs blink their bulging eyes to help them swallow food. The surinam toad has small eyes and no eyelids.

The surinam toad also looks very different from other frogs. It has a face shaped like a triangle. Its nostrils jut out from its nose. Most frogs are slim. The surinam toad is very, very slim. In fact, it is nearly flat.

The female surinam toad loses some of her flatness when she carries her eggs. The male frog puts the new eggs on the female's back. Covered up with the mother frog's bumpy skin, the eggs are safe. They will not float away. The eggs grow for three to four months. In some surinam toads, the eggs hatch into tadpoles. In others, they hatch as tiny frogs called froglets.

Surinam toads grow to about 7 inches (18 centimeters). That's about as big as an adult's hand. They live in the river bottoms of South America.

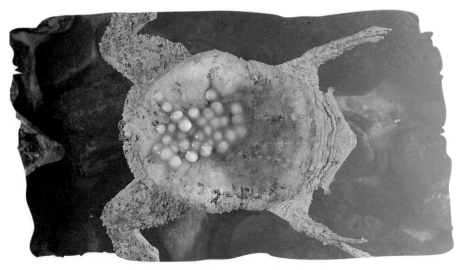

A female surinam toad carries eggs on her back.

A Mammal in Water

The manatee is a very large aquatic mammal that spends its whole life in the water. Manatees live in rivers and along coastlines where the water is fairly shallow. Just a few other mammals are fully aquatic. Other aquatic mammals are whales, porpoises, and dolphins.

The manatee has no enemies in the ocean. It eats only plants and is too large to be prey for other animals or fish. They range in weight from 440 pounds to more than 2,000 pounds (198–900 kilograms). To support their weight, they spend 6 to 8 hours eating each day. One large manatee may eat up to 200 pounds (90 kilograms) of plants in a day!

Manatees are shy, gentle creatures.

Flippers help manatees find food.

The manatee's two front flippers and broad, flat tail are its special features. It uses its flippers for steering as it swims. It also uses them to push itself along the bottom of its watery **habitat**. Special nails at the end of these flippers help the manatee grab plants when it is hungry. In shallow water, the manatee often sits on its tail. It swims by moving its tail up and down like a mermaid.

As a mammal, the manatee must breathe air. It has nostrils that close underwater. They open again when the manatee comes up to breathe every few minutes. Just the top of the manatee's snout needs to be above water for it to breathe. That is where its nostrils are. A manatee can hold its breath and stay underwater for up to ten minutes.

A newborn manatee is called a calf. It can weigh as much as 60 pounds (27 kilograms) when it is born. Manatees are born pink and become grayish as they age. Young manatees stay with their mothers for up to two years.

Manatees seem to be friendly. They like to be around other manatees. They often live together in small groups. They play with one another and make sounds as if they were talking. Some manatees have grown used to people. But most are careful and stay away from us.

Manatees live along the coasts of Florida, down into South America, and over into Africa. They live in warm waters. Some can live up to forty years.

Glossary

angler a fisher that uses a lure to catch prey

aquatic living in water

arboreal living mostly in trees

camouflage a way to hide or change appearance and blend in with the background

coral large ocean forms like rocks, but made of the tiny bones of sea creatures

dorsal fins the fins on a fish's back

environment the area and conditions around an animal

habitat the kind of place where an animal lives

nocturnal active during the night

pectoral fins the forward chest fins on a fish

predator an animal that catches other creatures for food

prey a creature that is caught by other animals for food

primates a class of animals that includes monkeys, apes, and humans

semiaquatic living some of the time in water

spiny having pointed, bony parts

venomous giving off venom; poisonous

Index